Easy

2 Hour Slippers

Volume 3

Fun Family Slippers

By

Vicki Becker

Copyright Information Page

Vicki Becker

www.vickisdesigns.com

First Printing, 2013

ISBN-13: 978-1491260241

ISBN-10: 1491260246

Printed in the United States of America

Contents

Introduction

These cute slippers are very quick and easy to make. The designs use #4 medium weight yarns. The pattern instructions include 5 styles of slippers for children and adults in six sizes.

The cute puppies, colorful owls, pink poodles, calico cats, and mischievous sock monkeys are all great for gift giving.

I hope you enjoy my pattern for these easy to crochet slippers.

General Instructions

Gauge

Gauge is determined by the tightness or looseness of your work and will affect the finished size of your project. Make a small section of the pattern before starting your project to check the gauge.

Understanding Symbols

As asterisk (*) indicates that the directions immediately following are to be repeated the given number of times in addition to the original.

Parenthesis is used to set off a group of instructions worked a number of times or in a particular stitch. For example, "(3 dc, ch 1, 3 dc) in each corner" or "(3 dc, ch 3) 3 times".

How to read patterns with multiple sizes

When crocheting or knitting a pattern with multiple sizes parentheses are often used to include additional information for other sizes. For example, if the instructions read chain 12 (14, 16), you would chain 12 for size small, 14 for medium, and 16 for large.

Motif Centers

After making a center ring I always crochet over the tail end of the yarn. I can then pull the end of the yarn to make a nice tight center.

Standard Yarn Weight System

Most yarn and thread now come with a weight number on the wrapper. I provide the weight number of the yarn or thread I used to design each pattern. This makes it much easier to make substitutions.

Helpful Hints

Changing Colors

To change color in single or double crochet you always work the last two loops on the hook off with the new color.

For single crochet, pull up a loop in the current color you are using, draw the new color through the last two loops on the hook to complete the single crochet stitch.

For double crochet, yarn over, pull up a loop in the current color you are using, draw through two loops, draw the new color through the last two loops on the hook to complete the double crochet stitch.

Size G Crochet Hook

Have you ever noticed that size G crochet hooks come in different millimeters? Depending on the manufacturer the size can be anywhere from 4.0mm to 4.5mm. The 4.5mm can also be called a size 7. If your gauge is just slightly off you may just need a different size G hook!

Make your slippers non-slip!

Knitted or crocheted slippers are very slippery on laminate, hard wood, or tile floors. There are several methods to make them non-slip.

I use Puffy Paint. You can find puffy paint just about anywhere that sells craft supplies. Just dot some on the slipper bottom or make some squiggly lines or swirls.

Available on-line is Regia ABS Latex or Efco Sock Stop.

Abbreviations

Abbreviations			
beg	beginning	rep (s)	repeat (s)
ch (s)	chain (s)	rnd (s)	round (s)
dc	double crochet	sc	single crochet
dtr	double treble crochet	sk	skip
hdc	half double crochet	sl st	slip stitch
lp (s)	loop (s)	sp (s)	space (s)
pat	pattern	st (s)	stitch (es)
rem	remaining	tr	treble crochet
		yo	yarn over

Crochet Terms

British vs American English Crochet Terms			
British English		**US - American English**	
Double Crochet	dc	Single Crochet	sc
Half Treble	htr	Half Double Crochet	hdc
Treble	tr	Double Crochet	dc
Double Treble	dtr	Treble	tr
Triple Treble	trtr	Double Treble	dtr
Miss		Skip	
Tension		Gauge	
Yarn Over Hook	yoh	Yarn Over	yo
All pattern instructions use US terms.			

Sock Monkey Slippers

Instructions

Sizes

Children - Small (12-13) 5 1/2", Medium (1-2) 6 1/2", Large (3-4) 7 1/2"

Adult - Small (5-6) 8 1/2", Medium (7-8) 9 1/2", Large (9-10) 10 1/2"

Materials: Red Heart yarns were use to make the slippers shown in the photos or you may use any number 4 yarn.

The children's slippers take small amounts and scrap yarns can be used.

Children's Sizes

Warm Brown - 1 ounce (28.4g)

Burgundy - 1/2 ounce (14.2g)

Soft White - 1/2 ounce (14.2g)

Adult Sizes

Warm Brown - 2 ounces (56.7g)

Burgundy - 1 ounce (28.4g)

Soft White - 1 ounce (28.4g)

For all sizes

4 Black Buttons - 1/2 inch for Children's slippers.

5/8 inch for Adult slippers.

Embroidery floss - Black and white.

Tapestry or yarn needle

Embroidery Needle

Hook: Size H (5.0mm) crochet hook or size to obtain gauge

Gauge: 4 dc = 1 inch 2 rows = 1 inch

Children's Sock Monkey Slippers

Instructions

Small

With Burgundy, ch 4, join with a sl st to form a ring.

Rnd 1: Ch 3. 9 dc in ring. Join with a sl st to top of first ch 3. 10 dc.

Rnd 2: Ch 1. 2 sc in same sp as last sl st. *2 sc in next st, rep from * around. Join with a sl st to first sc. 20 sc. Fasten off.

Rnd 3-4: Attach Soft White in same sp as sl st. Ch 3. 1 dc in each st around. Join with a sl st to top of first ch 3. 20 dc.

Rnd 5: Attach Warm Brown in same sp as sl st. Ch 3. 1 dc in each st around. Join with a sl st to top of first ch 3. 20 dc.

Note: *You will now be working in rows. Beginning Ch 3 counts for a dc now and throughout.*

Row 6: Ch 3. 1 dc in each of next 14 sts. Ch 3. Turn. 15 dc.

Rows 7-10: 1 dc in each of next 14 sts. Ch 3. Turn. 15 dc.

Row 11: 1 dc in each of next 5 sts. Work next 3 sts together as follows: (yo, insert hook in next st, draw up lp, yo, draw through 2 lps) 3 times, yo, draw through 4 lps on hook. 1 dc in each of next 6 sts. Fasten off leaving a length of yarn to sew center back of slipper. With yarn end threaded in tapestry needle sew slipper heel together.

Edging

Rnd 1: With Burgundy rejoin yarn with sc around bar of dc just to the left of heel. Sc around same bar. Sc evenly around top edge of slipper. Join with a sl st to first sc. Fasten off.

Drawstring (optional): Ch 60. Fasten off. Starting at heel weave through the top edge of slipper just under edging and through the dc's across the toe.

Ears (make 4):

Row 1: With Warm Brown ch 4. Sc in 2nd ch from hook, 3 dc in next ch, sc in last ch. Ch 1. Turn.

Row 2: Sc in each st across row (5 sc). Fasten off leaving a length of yarn to sew ear to slipper.

Finishing

Using the photo as a guide, sew two 1/2 inch black buttons with 3 strands of white embroidery floss for the monkey's eyes.

Note: *For children under 3 years of age you should exercise caution when using buttons for eyes. You can embroider the eyes with black embroidery floss instead.*

To embroider the money's nose use satin stitch and 3 strands of black embroidery floss. Sew ears to sides of face.

Medium (Large)

Note: *Numbers in parenthesis are for the children's large size.*

With Burgundy, Ch 4, join with a sl st to form a ring.

Rnd 1: Ch 3. 10 (11) dc in ring. Join with a sl st to top of first ch 3. 11 (12) dc.

Rnd 2: Ch 3. 1 dc in same sp as last sl st. 2 dc in each st around. 22 (24) dc. Fasten off.

Rnd 3-4: Attach Soft White in same sp as sl st. Ch 3. 1 dc in each st around. Join with a sl st to top of first ch 3. 22 (24) dc. Fasten off.

Rnd 5 (6): Attach Warm Brown in same sp as sl st. Ch 3. 1 dc in each st around. Join with a sl st to top of first ch 3. 22 (24) dc.

Note: *You will now be working in rows. Beginning Ch 3 counts for a dc now and throughout.*

Rows 6 (7): Ch 3. 1 dc in each of next 15 (17, 17) sts. Ch 3. Turn. 16 (18, 18) dc.

Rows 7-12 (8-13): 1 dc in each st across. Ch 3. Turn. 16 (18, 18) dc.

Row 13 (14): 1 dc in each of next 6 (7) sts. Work next 2 sts together as follows: (yo, insert hook in next st, draw up lp, yo, draw through 2 lps) 2 times, yo, draw through 3 lps on hook. 1 dc in each of next 7 (8) sts. Fasten off leaving a length of yarn to sew center back of slipper. With yarn end threaded in tapestry needle sew slipper heel together.

Edging

Rnd 1: With Burgundy rejoin yarn with sc around bar of dc just to the left of heel. Sc around same bar. Sc evenly around top edge of slipper. Join with a sl st to first sc. Fasten off.

Drawstring (optional): With Burgundy ch 70 (75). Fasten off. Starting at heel weave through the top edge of slipper just under edging and through the dc's across the toe. Tie in a bow at center back.

Ears (make 4):

Row 1: With Warm Brown, ch 4. Sc in 2nd ch from hook, 5 dc in next ch, sc in last ch. 7 sts. Ch 1. Turn.

Row 2: Sc in each st across row. 7 sc. Fasten off leaving a length of yarn to sew ear to slipper.

Finishing

Using the photo as a guide, sew two 1/2 inch black buttons using 3 strands of white embroidery floss for the monkey's eyes.

To embroider the money's nose use satin stitch and 3 strands of black embroidery floss. Sew ears to sides of face.

Adult Sock Monkey Slippers

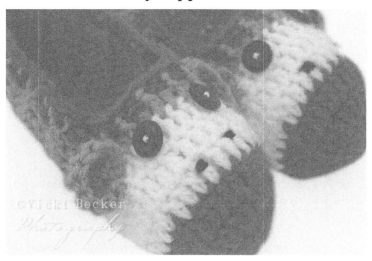

Instructions

Note: *Numbers in parenthesis are for medium and large sizes.*

With Burgundy, ch 4. Join with a sl st to form a ring.

Rnd 1: Ch 3. 11 dc in ring. Join with a sl st to top of first ch 3. 12 dc.

Rnd 2: Ch 3. 1 dc in same sp as last sl st. * 2 dc in next st, rep from * around. Join with a sl st to top of first ch 3. 24 dc.

Rnd 3: *For small size only.* Ch 3. 1 dc in same sp as last sl st. 1 dc in each of next 3 sts. *2 dc in next st. 1 dc in each of next 3 sts. Rep from * around. Join with a sl st to top of first ch 3. 30 dc. Fasten off.

Rnds 4-6: *For small size only.* Attach Soft White in same sp as sl st. Ch 3. 1 dc in each st around. Join with a sl st to top of first ch 3. 30 dc. Fasten off.

Rnd 7: *For small size only.* Attach Warm Brown in same sp as sl st. Ch 3. 1 dc in each st around. Join with a sl st to top of first ch 3. 30 dc.

Rnd 3: *For sizes medium and large.* Ch 3. 1 dc in same sp as last sl st. 1 dc in each of next 5 sts. *2 dc in next st. 1 dc in each of next 5 sts. Rep from * around. Join with a sl st to top of first ch 3. 28 dc. Fasten off.

Rnd 4: *For sizes medium and large.* Attach Soft White in same sp as sl st. Ch 3. 1 dc in same

Rnds 5-6: *For sizes medium and large.* Ch 3. 1 dc in each st around. Join with a sl st to top of first ch 3. 32 dc. Fasten off.

Rnd 7: *For sizes medium and large.* Attach Warm Brown in same sp as sl st. Ch 3. 1 dc in each st around. Join with a sl st to top of first ch 3.

Note: *You will now be working in rows for all sizes. Medium and Large instructions are in parenthesis. Beginning ch 3 counts for a dc now and throughout.*

Row 8: Ch 3. 1 dc in each of next 22 (24, 24) sts. Ch 3. Turn. 23 (25, 25) dc.

Rows 9-15 (16, 18): 1 dc in each st across. Ch 3. Turn. 23 (25, 25) dc.

Row 16 (17, 18): 1 dc in each of next 9 (10, 10) sts. Work next 3 sts together as follows: (yo, insert hook in next st, draw up lp, yo, draw through 2 lps) 3 times, yo, draw through 4 lps on hook. 1 dc in each of next 10 (11, 11) sts. Fasten off leaving a length of yarn to sew center back of slipper. With yarn end threaded in tapestry needle sew slipper heel together.

Edging

Rnd 1: With Burgundy rejoin yarn with sc around bar of dc just to the left of heel. Sc around same bar. 2 sc around each bar and 1 sc in each st across toe. Join with a sl st to first sc. Fasten off.

Drawstring (optional): With Burgundy ch 90. Fasten off. Starting at heel weave through the top edge of slipper just under edging and through the dc's across the toe. (see photo below) Tie in a bow at center back.

Ears (make 4):

Row 1: With Warm Brown ch 4. Sc in 2nd ch from hook, 5 dc in next ch, sc in last ch. Ch 1. Turn. 7 sts.

Row 2: Sc in first st, dc in next 5 sts, sc in last st. 7 sts. Fasten off leaving a length of yarn to sew ear to slipper.

Finishing

Using the photo as a guide, sew two 5/8 inch black buttons using 3 strands of white embroidery floss for the monkey's eyes.

To embroider the money's nose use satin stitch and 3 strands of black embroidery floss. Sew ears to sides of face.

Owl Slippers

Instructions

Sizes

Children - Small (12-13) 5 1/2", Medium (1-2), 6 1/2", Large (3-4) 7 1/2"

Adult - Small (5-6) 8 1/2" Medium (7-8) 9 1/2", Large (9-10) 10 1/2"

Materials: Red Heart yarns were use to make the slippers shown in the photos or you may use any number 4 yarn.

The children's slippers take small amounts and scrap yarns can be used.

Children's Sizes

Main Color - 1 ounce (28.4g)

Contrasting Color - 1/2 ounce (14.2g)

Small amounts of white, orange, and 2nd contrasting color.

Adult Sizes

Main Color - 2 ounces (56.7g)

Contrasting Color - 1 ounce (28.4g)

Small amounts of white, orange, and 2nd contrasting color.

For all sizes

4 Black Buttons - 5/8 inch for Children's slippers. 3/4 inch for Adult slippers.

Embroidery floss - Black

Tapestry or yarn needle

Embroidery Needle

Hook: Size H (5.0mm) crochet hook or size to obtain gauge.

Gauge: 4 dc = 1 inch 2 rows = 1 inch

Children's Owl Slippers

Instructions

Note: *Numbers in parenthesis are for medium and large sizes.*

With contrasting color ch 4. Join with a sl st to form a ring.

Rnd 1: Ch 3. 9 (10, 11) dc in ring. Join with a sl st to top of first ch 3. 10 (11, 12) dc.

Rnd 2: Ch 3. 1 dc in same sp as last sl st. 2 dc in each st around. 20 (22, 24) dc.

Rnd 3: Ch 3. 1 dc in each st around. Join with a sl st to top of first ch 3. 20 (22, 24) dc. Small and medium sizes only fasten off.

Rnd 4: *Small size only.* Attach main color in same sp as sl st. Ch 3. 1 dc in each st around. Join with a sl st to top of first ch 3. 20 dc.

Rnd 4-5: *Medium size only.* Attach main color in same sp as sl st. Ch 3. 1 dc in each st around. Join with a sl st to top of first ch 3. 22 dc.

Rnd 4: *Large size only.* Ch 3. 1 dc in each st around. Join with a sl st to top of first ch 3. 24 dc. Fasten off.

Rnd 5-6: *Large size only.* Attach main color in same sp as sl st. Ch 3. 1 dc in each st around. Join with a sl st to top of first ch 3. 24 dc.

Note: *You will now be working in rows. Medium and Large size instructions are in parenthesis. Beginning Ch 3 counts for a dc now and throughout.*

Rows 5 (6, 7): Ch 3. 1 dc in each of next 16 (18, 18) sts. Ch 3. Turn. 17 (19, 19) dc.

Rows 6-9 (7-12, 8-13): 1 dc in each st across. Ch 3. Turn. 17 (19, 19) dc.

Row 10 (13, 14): 1 dc in each of next 6 (7, 7) sts. Work next 2 sts together as follows: (yo, insert hook in next st, draw up lp, yo, draw through 2 lps) 2 times, yo, draw through 3 lps on hook. 1 dc in each of next 7 (8, 8) sts. Fasten off leaving a length of yarn to sew center back of slipper. With yarn end threaded in tapestry needle sew slipper heel together.

Edging

Rnd 1: With 2nd contrasting color rejoin yarn with sc around bar of dc just to the left of heel. Sc around same bar. Sc evenly around top edge of slipper. Join with a sl st to first sc. Fasten off.

Drawstring (optional): With main color ch 65 (70, 75). Fasten off. Starting at heel weave through the top edge of slipper just under edging and through the dc's across the toe. Tie in a bow at center back.

Eyes (make 4): With white ch 4. Join with a sl st to form a ring.

Rnd 1: *Small size only.* Ch 1. 12 sc in ring. Join to first sc. 12 sc. Fasten off leaving a length of yarn to sew eyes to slipper.

Rnd 1: *Medium and Large sizes only.* Ch 2. 11 hdc in ring. 12 hdc. Join with a sl st to top of first ch 3. Fasten off leaving a length of yarn to sew eyes to slipper.

Beak (make 2): With orange ch 4.

Row 1: Sc in 2nd ch from hook. Sc in next 2 chs. Ch 1. Turn.

Row 2: Work next 3 sts together as follows: insert hook in next st, draw up lp, 3 times, yo draw through 4 lps on hook. Ch 1. Fasten off leaving a length of yarn to sew beak to slipper.

Flower (optional): With color of your choice ch 4. Join with a sl st to form a ring.

Rnd 1: *Ch 3, 2 dc, ch 3, sl st in ring. Rep from * 4 times. Fasten off. 5 Petals. Make one for each slipper.

Finishing

Using the photo as a guide, sew the two white eye circles in place. Sew two 5/8 inch black buttons using 3 strands of black embroidery floss on top of the white circles for the owl's eyes.

Note: *For children under 3 years of age you should exercise caution when using buttons for eyes. You can embroider the eyes with black embroidery floss instead.*

Stitch beak in place. Cut 12 pieces of assorted yarn about 8 inches long for fringe. Attach fringe to slipper edging as shown in photograph. Trim fringe to 1 1/2 inches.

Sew flowers in place if desired.

Adult Owl Slippers

Instructions

Note: *Numbers in parenthesis are for medium and large sizes.*

With contrasting color, ch 4. Join with a sl st to form a ring.

Rnd 1: Ch 3. 11 dc in ring. Join with a sl st to top of first ch 3. 12 dc.

Rnd 2: Ch 3. 1 dc in same sp as last sl st. * 2 dc in next st, rep from * around. Join with a sl st to top of first ch 3. 24 dc.

Rnd 3: *For small size only.* Ch 3. 1 dc in same sp as last sl st. 1 dc in each of next 3 sts. *2 dc in next st. 1 dc in each of next 3 sts. Rep from * around. Join with a sl st to top of first ch 3. 30 dc.

Rnd 4: *For small size only.* Ch 3. 1 dc in each st around. Join with a sl st to top of first ch 3. 30 dc. Fasten off.

Rnds 5-7: *For small size only.* Attach main color in same sp as sl st. Ch 3. 1 dc in each st around. Join with a sl st to top of first ch 3. 30 dc.

Rnd 3: *For sizes medium and large.* Ch 3. 1 dc in same sp as last sl st. 1 dc in each of next 5 sts. *2 dc in next st. 1 dc in each of next 5 sts. Rep from * around. Join with a sl st to top of first ch 3. 28 dc. Fasten off.

Rnd 4: *For sizes medium and large.* Ch 3. 1 dc in same sp as last sl st. 1 dc in each of next 6 sts. *2 dc in next st. 1 dc in each of next 6 sts. Rep from * around. Join with a sl st to top of first ch 3. 32 dc. Fasten off.

Rnds 5-7: *For sizes medium and large.* Attach main color in same sp as sl st. Ch 3. 1 dc in each st around. Join with a sl st to top of first ch 3. 32 dc.

Note: *You will now be working in rows for all sizes. Medium and Large instructions are in parenthesis. Beginning Ch 3 counts for a dc now and throughout.*

Row 8: Ch 3. 1 dc in each of next 22 (24, 24) sts. Ch 3. Turn. 23 (25, 25) dc.

Rows 9-15 (16, 18): 1 dc in each st across. Ch 3. Turn. 23 (25, 25) dc.

Row 16 (17, 18): 1 dc in each of next 9 (10, 10) sts. Work next 3 sts together as follows: (yo, insert hook in next st, draw up lp, yo, draw through 2 lps) 3 times, yo, draw through 4 lps on hook. 1 dc in each of next 10 (11, 11) sts. Fasten off leaving a length of yarn to sew center back of slipper. With yarn end threaded in tapestry needle sew slipper heel together.

Edging

Rnd 1: With 2nd contrasting color rejoin yarn with sc around bar of dc just to the left of heel. Sc around same bar.

2 sc around each bar and 1 sc in each st across toe. Join with a sl st to first sc. Fasten off.

Drawstring (optional): With main color ch 90. Fasten off. Starting at heel weave through the top edge of slipper just under edging and through the dc's across the toe. Tie in a bow at center back.

Eyes (make 4): With white ch 4. Join with a sl st to form a ring.

Rnd 1: Ch 3. 11 dc in ring. 12 dc. Join with a sl st to top of first ch 3. Fasten off leaving a length of yarn to sew eyes to slipper.

Beak (make 2): With orange ch 4.

Row 1: Sc in 2nd ch from hook. Sc in next 2 chs. Ch 1. Turn.

Row 2: Sc in each st across row. 3 sc. Ch 1. Turn.

Row 3: Work next 3 sts together as follows: insert hook in next st, draw up lp, 3 times, yo draw through 4 lps on hook. Ch 1. Fasten off leaving a length of yarn to sew beak to slipper.

Flower (optional): With color of your choice ch 4. Join with a sl st to form a ring.

Rnd 1: *Ch 3, 2 dc, ch 3, sl st in ring. Rep from * 4 times. Fasten off. 5 Petals. Make one for each slipper.

Finishing

Using the photo as a guide, sew the two white eye circles in place. Sew two 7/8 inch black buttons using 3 strands of black embroidery floss on top of the white circles for the owl's eyes.

Stitch beak in place. Cut 12 pieces of assorted yarn about 8 inches long for fringe. Attach fringe to slipper edging as shown in photograph. Trim fringe to 1 1/2 inches.

Pink Poodle Slippers

Instructions

Sizes

Children - Small (12-13) 5 1/2", Medium (1-2) 6 1/2", Large (3-4) 7 1/2"

Adult - Small (5-6) 8 1/2", Medium (7-8) 9 1/2", Large (9-10) 10 1/2"

Materials: Red Heart yarns were use to make the slippers shown in the photos or you may use any number 4 yarn.

Children's Sizes

Petal Pink - 1.5 ounce (42.6g)

Small amount of black for nose.

Adult Sizes

Petal Pink - 2.5 ounces (70.9g)

Small amount of black for nose.

For all sizes

4 Black Buttons - 5/8 inch for Children's slippers. 3/4 inch for Adult slippers.

Embroidery floss – Black

Tapestry or yarn needle

Embroidery Needle

Hook: Size H (5.0mm) crochet hook or size to obtain gauge

Gauge: 4 dc = 1 inch 2 rows = 1 inch

Children's Pink Poodle Slippers

Instructions

Note: You can make the poodle's nose two different ways. The instructions below are for the nose to be crocheted in the first rnd. You can also make the nose separately and then sew it on. If you would like to make the nose separately start the slipper with pink and complete following the directions. Then using black yarn, crochet rnd 1 and fasten off leaving a tail of yarn to sew the nose to poodle. In the photo above the slipper on the right is crocheted in and the slipper on the left is stitched on. I think the stitched on method gives more depth.

Note: *Numbers in parenthesis are for medium and large sizes.*

With black, ch 4. Join with a sl st to form a ring.

Rnd 1: Ch 3. 9 (10, 11) dc in ring. Join with a sl st to top of first ch 3. 10 (11, 12) dc. Fasten off.

Rnd 2: Attach Petal Pink in same sp as sl st. Ch 3. 1 dc in each st around. Join with a sl st to top of first ch 3. 20 (22, 24) dc.

Rnd 3-4 (5, 6): Ch 3. 1 dc in each st around. Join with a sl st to top of first ch 3. 20 (22, 24) dc.

Note: *You will now be working in rows. Medium and Large size instructions are in parenthesis. Beginning Ch 3 counts for a dc now and throughout.*

Rows 5 (6, 7): Ch 3. 1 dc in each of next 16 (18, 18) sts. Ch 3. Turn. 17 (19, 19) dc.

Rows 6-9 (7-12, 8-13): 1 dc in each st across. Ch 3. Turn. 17 (19, 19) dc.

Row 10 (13, 14): 1 dc in each of next 6 (7, 7) sts. Work next 2 sts together as follows: (yo, insert hook in next st, draw up lp, yo, draw through 2 lps) 2 times, yo, draw through 3 lps on hook. 1 dc in each of next 7 (8, 8) sts. Fasten off leaving a length of yarn to sew center back of slipper. With yarn end threaded in tapestry needle sew slipper heel together.

Edging

Rnd 1: With Petal Pink rejoin yarn with sc around bar of dc just to the left of heel. Sc around same bar. Sc evenly around top edge of slipper. Join with a sl st to first sc. Fasten off.

Drawstring (optional): With Petal Pink ch 65 (70, 75). Fasten off. Starting at heel weave through the top edge of slipper just under edging and through the dc's across the toe. Tie in a bow at center back.

Ears (Make 4):

With Petal Pink, ch 6 (7, 7). Leave a tail of yarn to sew ears to poodle before starting your chain.

Row 1: Sc in 2nd ch from hook and in each ch across. Ch 1. Turn. 5 (6, 6) sc.

Rows 2-5 (6, 6): Sc in each st across. Ch 1. Turn. 5 (6, 6) sc.

Row 6 (7, 7): Work first 2 sts together as follows: insert hook in next st, draw up lp, 2 times, yo, draw through 3 lps on hook. Sc in next 1 (2, 2) sts. Work last 2 sts together. Ch 1. Turn.

Row 7: *For small size only.* Work remaining 3 sts together as follows: insert hook in next st, draw up lp, 3 times, yo, draw through 4 lps on hook. Ch 1. Fasten off leaving a length of yarn to sew ear to slipper.

Row 7: *For medium and large sizes only.* Work first 2 sts together as follows: insert hook in next st, draw up lp, 2 times, yo, draw through 3 lps on hook. Sc in next st. Work last 2 sts together. Ch 1. Turn.

Row 8: *For medium and large sizes only.* Work remaining 3 sts together as follows: insert hook in next st, draw up lp, 3 times, yo, draw through 4 lps on hook. Ch 1. Fasten off.

Finishing

Weave in all loose ends. Using the photo as a guide, sew two 5/8 inch black buttons using 3 strands of black embroidery floss for poodle's eyes.

Note: *For children under 3 years of age you should exercise caution when using buttons for eyes. You can embroider the eyes with black embroidery floss instead.*

Cut 25 pieces of Petal Pink yarn about 6 inches long for fringe. Wrap a 6 inch length of yarn around the center of the fringe and knot tightly. Sew the center of the fringe bundle to the center of the slipper just below the edging as shown in the photograph. Trim fringe to 1 1/2 - 2 inches depending on the size of the slipper.

Sew ears to the side of the slipper above the drawstring on the edging.

Adult Pink Poodle Slippers

Instructions

Note*: You can make the poodle's nose two different ways. The instructions below are for the nose to be crocheted in the first rnd. You can also make the nose separately and then sew it on. If you would like to make the nose separately start the slipper with pink and complete following the directions. Then using black yarn, crochet rnd 1 and fasten off leaving a tail of yarn to sew the nose to poodle. In the photo above the nose is stitched on. I think the stitched on method gives more depth.*

Note: *Numbers in parenthesis are for medium and large sizes.*

With black, ch 4. Join with a sl st to form a ring.

Rnd 1: Ch 3. 11 dc in ring. Join with a sl st to top of first ch 3. 12 dc. Fasten off.

Rnd 2: Attach Petal Pink in same sp as sl st. Ch 3. 1 dc in same sp as last sl st. * 2 dc in next st, rep from * around. Join with a sl st to top of first ch 3. 24 dc.

Rnd 3: *For small size only.* Ch 3. 1 dc in same sp as last sl st. 1 dc in each of next 3 sts. *2 dc in next st. 1 dc in each of next 3 sts. Rep from * around. Join with a sl st to top of first ch 3. 30 dc.

Rnd 4-7: *For small size only.* Ch 3. 1 dc in each st around. Join with a sl st to top of first ch 3. 30 dc.

Rnd 3: *For sizes medium and large.* Ch 3. 1 dc in same sp as last sl st. 1 dc in each of next 5 sts. *2 dc in next st. 1 dc in each of next 5 sts. Rep from * around. Join with a sl st to top of first ch 3. 28 dc. Fasten off.

Rnd 4: *For sizes medium and large.* Ch 3. 1 dc in same sp as last sl st. 1 dc in each of next 6 sts. *2 dc in next st. 1 dc in each of next 6 sts. Rep from * around. Join with a sl st to top of first ch 3. 32 dc.

Rnds 5-7*: For sizes medium and large.* Ch 3. 1 dc in each st around. Join with a sl st to top of first ch 3. 32 dc.

Note: *You will now be working in rows for all sizes. Medium and Large instructions are in parenthesis. Beginning Ch 3 counts for a dc now and throughout.*

Row 8: Ch 3. 1 dc in each of next 22 (24, 24) sts. Ch 3. Turn. 23 (25, 25) dc.

Rows 9-15 (16, 18): 1 dc in each st across. Ch 3. Turn. 23 (25, 25) dc.

Row 16 (17, 18): 1 dc in each of next 9 (10, 10) sts. Work next 3 sts together as follows: (yo, insert hook in next st, draw up lp, yo, draw through 2 lps) 3 times, yo, draw through 4 lps on hook. 1 dc in each of next 10 (11, 11) sts. Fasten off leaving a length of yarn to sew center back of slipper. With yarn end threaded in tapestry needle sew slipper heel together.

Edging

Rnd 1: With Petal Pink rejoin yarn with sc around bar of dc just to the left of heel. Sc around same bar. 2 sc around each bar and 1 sc in each st across toe. Join with a sl st to first sc. Fasten off.

Drawstring (optional): With Petal Pink ch 90. Fasten off. Starting at heel weave through the top edge of slipper just under edging and through the dc's across the toe. Tie in a bow at center back.

Ears (Make 4):

With Petal Pink, ch 8. Leave a tail of yarn to sew ears to poodle before starting your chain.

Row 1: Sc in 2nd ch from hook and in each ch across. Ch 1. Turn. 7 sc.

Rows 2-9: Sc in each st across. Ch 1. Turn. 7 sc.

Row 10: Work first 2 sts together as follows: insert hook in next st, draw up lp, 2 times, draw through 3 lps on hook. Sc in next 3 sts. Work last 2 sts together. Ch 1. Turn.

Row 11: Work first 2 sts together as follows: insert hook in next st, draw up lp, 2 times, yo, draw through 3 lps on hook. Sc in next st. Work last 2 sts together the same way. Ch 1. Turn.

Row 12: Work remaining 3 sts together as follows: insert hook in next st, draw up lp, 3 times, yo, draw through 4 lps on hook. Ch 1. Fasten off.

Finishing

Weave in all loose ends. Using the photo as a guide, sew two 3/4 inch black buttons using 3 strands of black embroidery floss for poodle's eyes.

Cut 25 pieces of Petal Pink yarn about 6 inches long for fringe. Wrap a 6 inch length of yarn around the center of the fringe and knot tightly. Sew the center of the fringe bundle to the center of the slipper just below the edging as shown in the photograph. Trim fringe to 1 1/2 - 2 inches depending on the size of the slipper.

Sew ears to the side of the slipper above the drawstring on the edging.

Calico Cat Slippers

Instructions

Sizes

Children - Small (12-13) 5 1/2", Medium (1-2), 6 1/2", Large (3-4) 7 1/2"

Adult - Small (5-6) 8 1/2", Medium (7-8) 9 1/2", Large (9-10) 10 1/2"

Materials: Loops & Threads Impeccable yarns (Available at Michaels) were use to make the slippers shown in the photos or you may use any number 4 yarn.

Children's Sizes

Color 02009 Stillness - 1.5 ounce (42.6g)

Adult Sizes

Color 02009 Stillness - 2.5 ounces (70.9g)

For all sizes

Wiggle Eyes - Adult: 20mm. Children's: 12mm (I purchased the eyes in the photo at Michaels).

Note: *Not recommended for children under 3 years of age. Embroider eyes for young children.*

Clear Gel Tacky Glue

Fray Check

Embroidery floss - Brown and White

Tapestry or yarn needle

Embroidery Needle

Hook: Size H (5.0mm) crochet hook or size to obtain gauge

Gauge: 4 dc = 1 inch 2 rows = 1 inch

Children's Calico Cat Slippers

Instructions

Note: *Numbers in parenthesis are for medium and large sizes.*

With Stillness, ch 4. Join with a sl st to form a ring.

Rnd 1: Ch 3. 9 (10, 11) dc in ring. Join with a sl st to top of first ch 3. 10 (11, 12) dc.

Rnd 2: Ch 3. 1 dc in same sp as last sl st. 2 dc in each st around. 20 (22, 24) dc.

Rnd 3-4 (5, 6): Ch 3. 1 dc in each st around. Join with a sl st to top of first ch 3. 20 (22, 24) dc.

Note: *You will now be working in rows. Medium and Large size instructions are in parenthesis. Beginning Ch 3 counts for a dc now and throughout.*

Rows 5 (6, 7): Ch 3. 1 dc in each of next 16 (18, 18) sts. Ch 3. Turn. 17 (19, 19) dc.

Rows 6-9 (7-12, 8-13): 1 dc in each st across. Ch 3. Turn. 17 (19, 19) dc.

Row 10 (13, 14): 1 dc in each of next 6 (7, 7) sts. Work next 2 sts together as follows: (yo, insert hook in next st, draw up lp, yo, draw through 2 lps) 2 times, yo, draw through 3 lps on hook. 1 dc in each of next 7 (8, 8) sts. Fasten off leaving a length of yarn to sew center back of slipper. With yarn end threaded in tapestry needle sew slipper heel together.

Edging

Rnd 1: With Stillness rejoin yarn with sc around bar of dc just to the left of heel. Sc around same bar. Sc evenly around top edge of slipper. Join with a sl st to first sc. Fasten off.

Drawstring (optional): With Stillness, ch 65 (70, 75). Fasten off. Starting at heel weave through the top edge of slipper just under edging and through the dc's across the toe. Tie in a bow at center back.

Ears (Make 4):

With Stillness, ch 2.

Note: *Work in rounds do not join. Mark beginning stitch with a contrasting piece of yarn, stitch marker, or safety pin.*

Rnd 1: 6 sc in 2nd ch from hook.

Rnd 2: *1 sc, 2 sc in next sc, repeat 3 times. (9 sc)

Rnd 3: Sc in each st around. Fasten off for small size leaving a length of yarn to sew ear to head. (9 sc)

Rnds 4: Sc in each st around. Fasten off for medium size leaving a length of yarn to sew ear to head. (9 sc)

Rnd 5: Sc in each st around. Fasten off for large size leaving a length of yarn to sew ear to head. (9 sc)

Finishing

Weave in all loose ends. Using the photo as a guide, glue wiggle eyes on face or embroider eyes. Using 6 strands of brown floss, embroider nose and mouth. For whiskers use 6 strands of white embroidery floss. Secure floss on wrong side of cats face and draw through to the front. Stiffen whiskers with fray check. **Note:** I put a few drops of fray check on my fingers and run the whiskers through my fingers.

Note: *For children under 3 years of age you should exercise caution when using buttons for eyes. You can embroider the eyes with black embroidery floss instead.*

Sew ears on face just above the eyes.

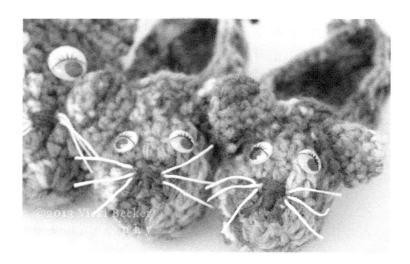

Adult Calico Cat Slippers

Instructions

Note: *Numbers in parenthesis are for medium and large sizes.*

With Stillness, ch 4. Join with a sl st to form a ring.

Rnd 1: Ch 3. 11 dc in ring. Join with a sl st to top of first ch 3. 12 dc. Fasten off.

Rnd 2: Ch 3. 1 dc in same sp as last sl st. * 2 dc in next st, rep from * around. Join with a sl st to top of first ch 3. 24 dc.

Rnd 3*: For small size only.* Ch 3. 1 dc in same sp as last sl st. 1 dc in each of next 3 sts. *2 dc in next st. 1 dc in each of next 3 sts. Rep from * around. Join with a sl st to top of first ch 3. 30 dc.

Rnd 4-7: *For small size only.* Ch 3. 1 dc in each st around. Join with a sl st to top of first ch 3. 30 dc.

Rnd 3: *For sizes medium and large.* Ch 3. 1 dc in same sp as last sl st. 1 dc in each of next 5 sts. *2 dc in next st. 1 dc in each of next 5 sts. Rep from * around. Join with a sl st to top of first ch 3. 28 dc. Fasten off.

Rnd 4: *For sizes medium and large.* Ch 3. 1 dc in same sp as last sl st. 1 dc in each of next 6 sts. *2 dc in next st. 1 dc in each of next 6 sts. Rep from * around. Join with a sl st to top of first ch 3. 32 dc.

Rnds 5-7: *For sizes medium and large.* Ch 3. 1 dc in each st around. Join with a sl st to top of first ch 3. 32 dc.

Note: *You will now be working in rows for all sizes. Medium and Large instructions are in parenthesis. Beginning Ch 3 counts for a dc now and throughout.*

Row 8: Ch 3. 1 dc in each of next 22 (24, 24) sts. Ch 3. Turn. 23 (25, 25) dc.

Rows 9-15 (16, 18): 1 dc in each st across. Ch 3. Turn. 23 (25, 25) dc.

Row 16 (17, 18): 1 dc in each of next 9 (10, 10) sts. Work next 3 sts together as follows: (yo, insert hook in next st, draw up lp, yo, draw through 2 lps) 3 times, yo, draw through 4 lps on hook. 1 dc in each of next 10 (11, 11) sts. Fasten off leaving a length of yarn to sew center back of slipper. With yarn end threaded in tapestry needle sew slipper heel together.

Edging

Rnd 1: With Stillness rejoin yarn with sc around bar of dc just to the left of heel. Sc around same bar. 2 sc around each bar and 1 sc in each st across toe. Join with a sl st to first sc. Fasten off.

Drawstring (optional): With Stillness, ch 90. Fasten off. Starting at heel weave through the top edge of slipper just under edging and through the dc's across the toe. Tie in a bow at center back.

Ears (Make 4):

With Stillness, ch 2.

Note: *Work in rounds do not join. Mark beginning stitch with a contrasting piece of yarn, stitch marker, or safety pin.*

Rnd 1: 6 sc in 2nd ch from hook.

Rnd 2: *1 sc, 2 sc in next sc, repeat 3 times. (9 sc)

Rnd 3: *2 sc, 2 sc in next sc, repeat 3 times. (12 sc)

Rnds 4-5: Sc in each st around. (12 sc)

Rnd 6: Sc in each st around. Fasten off leaving a length of yarn to sew ears to head. (12 sc)

Finishing

Weave in all loose ends. Using the photo as a guide, glue wiggle eyes on face or embroider eyes. Using 6 strands of brown floss, embroider nose and mouth. For whiskers use 6 strands of white embroidery floss. Secure floss on wrong side of cats face and draw through to the front. Stiffen whiskers with fray check. **Note:** *I put a few drops of fray check on my fingers and run the whiskers through my fingers.*

Sew ears on face just above the eyes.

Puppy Slippers

Instructions

Sizes

Children - Small (12-13) 5 1/2", Medium (1-2) 6 1/2", Large (3-4) 7 1/2"

Adult - Small (5-6) 8 1/2", Medium (7-8) 9 1/2", Large (9-10) 10 1/2"

Materials: Red Heart yarns were use to make the slippers shown in the photos or you may use any number 4 yarn.

Children's Sizes

Buff - 1.5 ounce (42.6g)

Small amount of black for nose. Small amount of Country Blue for edging, drawstring, and eye patch.

Adult Sizes

Buff - 2.5 ounces (70.9g)

Small amount of black for nose. Small amount of Country Blue for edging, drawstring, and eye patch.

For all sizes

4 Black Buttons - 5/8 inch for Children's slippers. 3/4 inch for Adult slippers.

Embroidery floss - Black

Tapestry or yarn needle

Embroidery Needle

Hook: Size H (5.0mm) crochet hook or size to obtain gauge

Gauge: 4 dc = 1 inch 2 rows = 1 inch

Children's Puppy Slippers

Instructions

Note: *You can make the puppy's nose two different ways. The instructions below are for the nose to be crocheted in the first rnd. You can also make the nose separately and then sew it on. If you would like to make the nose separately start the slipper with buff and complete following the directions. Then using black yarn, crochet rnd 1 and fasten off leaving a tail of yarn to sew the nose to the puppy. In the photo above the nose is stitched on. I think the stitched on method gives more depth.*

Note: *Numbers in parenthesis are for medium and large sizes*

With black, ch 4. Join with a sl st to form a ring.

Rnd 1: Ch 3. 9 (10, 11) dc in ring. Join with a sl st to top of first ch 3. 10 (11, 12) dc. Fasten off.

Rnd 2: Attach Buff in same sp as sl st. Ch 3. 1 dc in same sp as last sl st. 2 dc in each st around. 20 (22, 24) dc.

Rnd 3-4 (5, 6): Ch 3. 1 dc in each st around. Join with a sl st to top of first ch 3. 20 (22, 24) dc.

Note: *You will now be working in rows. Medium and Large size instructions are in parenthesis. Beginning Ch 3 counts for a dc now and throughout.*

Rows 5 (6, 7): Ch 3. 1 dc in each of next 16 (18, 18) sts. Ch 3. Turn. 17 (19, 19) dc.

Rows 6-9 (7-12, 8-13): 1 dc in each st across. Ch 3. Turn. 17 (19, 19) dc.

Row 10 (13, 14): 1 dc in each of next 6 (7, 7) sts. Work next 2 sts together as follows: (yo, insert hook in next st, draw up lp, yo, draw through 2 lps) 2 times, yo, draw through 3 lps on hook. 1 dc in each of next 7 (8, 8) sts. Fasten off leaving a length of yarn to sew center back of slipper. With yarn end threaded in tapestry needle sew slipper heel together.

Edging

Rnd 1: With Country Blue rejoin yarn with sc around bar of dc just to the left of heel. Sc around same bar. Sc evenly around top edge of slipper. Join with a sl st to first sc. Fasten off.

Drawstring (optional): With Country Blue, ch 65 (70, 75). Fasten off. Starting at heel weave through the top edge of slipper just under edging and through the dc's across the toe. Tie in a bow at center back.

Ears (Make 4):

With Buff, ch 6 (7, 7). Leave a tail of yarn to sew ears to puppy before starting your chain.

Row 1: Sc in 2nd ch from hook and in each ch across. Ch 1. Turn. 5 (6, 6) sc.

Rows 2-5 (6, 6): Sc in each st across. Ch 1. Turn. 5 (6, 6) sc.

Row 6 (7, 7): Work first 2 sts together as follows: insert hook in next st, draw up lp, 2 times, yo, draw through 3 lps on hook. Sc in next 1 (2, 2) sts. Work last 2 sts together. Ch 1. Turn.

Row 7: *For small size only.* Work remaining 3 sts together as follows: insert hook in next st, draw up lp, 3 times, yo, draw through 4 lps on hook. Ch 1. Fasten off leaving a length of yarn to sew ear to slipper.

Row 7*: For medium and large sizes only.* Work first 2 sts together as follows: insert hook in next st, draw up lp, 2 times, yo, draw through 3 lps on hook. Sc in next st. Work last 2 sts together. Fasten off.

Eye Patch (Make 2): With Country Blue ch 4. Join with a sl st to form a ring.

Rnd 1: *Small size only.* Ch 1. 12 sc in ring. Join to first sc. 12 sc. Fasten off leaving a length of yarn to sew eyes to slipper.

Rnd 1: *Medium and Large sizes only.* Ch 2. 11 hdc in ring. 12 hdc. Join with a sl st to top of first ch 3. Fasten off leaving a length of yarn to sew eyes to slipper.

Finishing

Weave in all loose ends. Using the photo as a guide, sew two 5/8 inch black buttons using 3 strands of black embroidery floss for puppy's eyes.

Note: *For children under 3 years of age you should exercise caution when using buttons for eyes. You can embroider the eyes with black embroidery floss instead.*

Sew ears to the side of the slipper just below the drawstring.

Adult Puppy Slippers

Note: *You can make the puppy's nose two different ways. The instructions below are for the nose to be crocheted in the first rnd. You can also make the nose separately and then sew it on. If you would like to make the nose separately start the slipper with buff and complete following the directions. Then using black yarn, crochet rnd 1 and fasten off leaving a tail of yarn to sew the nose to the puppy. In the photo above the nose is stitched on. I think the stitched on method gives more depth*

Note: *Numbers in parenthesis are for medium and large sizes*

With black, ch 4. Join with a sl st to form a ring.

Rnd 1: Ch 3. 11 dc in ring. Join with a sl st to top of first ch 3. 12 dc. Fasten off.

Rnd 2: Attach Buff in same sp as sl st. Ch 3. 1 dc in same sp as last sl st. * 2 dc in next st, rep from * around. Join with a sl st to top of first ch 3. 24 dc.

Rnd 3: For small size only. Ch 3. 1 dc in same sp as last sl st. 1 dc in each of next 3 sts. *2 dc in next st. 1 dc in each of next 3 sts. Rep from * around. Join with a sl st to top of first ch 3. 30 dc.

Rnd 4-7: *For small size only.* Ch 3. 1 dc in each st around. Join with a sl st to top of first ch 3. 30 dc.

Rnd 3: *For sizes medium and large.* Ch 3. 1 dc in same sp as last sl st. 1 dc in each of next 5 sts. *2 dc in next st. 1 dc in each of next 5 sts. Rep from * around. Join with a sl st to top of first ch 3. 28 dc. Fasten off.

Rnd 4: *For sizes medium and large.* Ch 3. 1 dc in same sp as last sl st. 1 dc in each of next 6 sts. *2 dc in next st. 1 dc in each of next 6 sts. Rep from * around. Join with a sl st to top of first ch 3. 32 dc.

Rnds 5-7: *For sizes medium and large.* Ch 3. 1 dc in each st around. Join with a sl st to top of first ch 3. 32 dc.

Note: *You will now be working in rows for all sizes. Medium and Large instructions are in parenthesis. Beginning Ch 3 counts for a dc now and throughout.*

Row 8: Ch 3. 1 dc in each of next 22 (24, 24) sts. Ch 3. Turn. 23 (25, 25) dc.

Rows 9-15 (16, 18): 1 dc in each st across. Ch 3. Turn. 23 (25, 25) dc.

Row 16 (17, 18): 1 dc in each of next 9 (10, 10) sts. Work next 3 sts together as follows: (yo, insert hook in next st, draw up lp, yo, draw through 2 lps) 3 times, yo, draw through 4 lps on hook. 1 dc in each of next 10 (11, 11) sts. Fasten off leaving a length of yarn to sew center back of slipper. With yarn end threaded in tapestry needle sew slipper heel together.

Edging

Rnd 1: With Country Blue rejoin yarn with sc around bar of dc just to the left of heel. Sc around same bar. 2 sc around each bar and 1 sc in each st across toe. Join with a sl st to first sc. Fasten off.

Drawstring (optional): With Country Blue, ch 90. Fasten off. Starting at heel weave through the top edge of slipper just under edging and through the dc's across the toe. Tie in a bow at center back.

Ears (Make 4):

With Buff, ch 8. Leave a tail of yarn to sew ears to puppy before starting your chain.

Row 1: Sc in 2nd ch from hook and in each ch across. Ch 1. Turn. 7 sc.

Rows 2-9: Sc in each st across. Ch 1. Turn. 7 sc.

Row 10: Work first 2 sts together as follows: insert hook in next st, draw up lp, 2 times, draw through 3 lps on hook. Sc in next 3 sts. Work last 2 sts together. Ch 1. Turn.

Row 11: Work first 2 sts together as follows: insert hook in next st, draw up lp, 2 times, yo, draw through 3 lps on hook. Sc in next st. Work last 2 sts together the same way. Fasten off.

Eye Patch (Make 2): With Country Blue, ch 4. Join with a sl st to form a ring.

Rnd 1: Ch 3. 11 dc in ring. 12 dc. Join with a sl st to top of first ch 3. Fasten off leaving a length of yarn to sew eye patch to slipper.

Finishing

Weave in all loose ends. Using the photo as a guide, sew two 3/4 inch black buttons using 3 strands of black embroidery floss for puppy's eyes.

Sew ears to the side of the slipper just below the drawstring.

Conclusion

I hope you enjoyed the patterns. Please consider leaving me a review. I value your opinion and would love to hear from you.

You can also visit my facebook fan page to leave a message or comment.

http://www.facebook.com/VickiBeckerAuthor

Visit my author page at Amazon for a list of my other needlework titles!

http://www.amazon.com/-/e/B009ZWK7Q6

Visit my web site for more needlework tips and free patterns!

http://vickisdesigns.com

You can email me

vicki@vickisdesigns.com